Happy With

ありのままが幸せ

By Marisa J. Taylor

Illustrated by Vanessa Balleza

BILINGUAL

English - Japanese

I love the color of my skin. I am unique and beautiful within.

わたしはじぶんのはだの色がだいすき。たった一人
のわたし、ありのままのわたしがすき。

I take pride in who I am and what I can do.

わたしでいること、わたしができることにじしんを持ってるの

Being me makes me happy from within.

わたしでいられることに幸^{しあわ}せをかんじるの。

I love to sing, dance and play with my friends, but that is just me, that makes me happy.

わたしは、うたったり、お友だちとあそんだりしてる時が幸せ。

What about you?   What makes you happy?

あなたはどう?何をしているときが幸せ?

Some of my friends love to play with toys and make a lot of noise. That is okay too, because to them it brings joy.

あるお友<ruby>友<rt>とも</rt></ruby>だちは、おもちゃであそんだり、さわいだりするのがすきなんだって。それもいいね。

Some of my friends love to sing, dance and chat away. That's okay, because everyone is different and special in their own way.

ほかのお友達<ruby>友達<rt>ともだち</rt></ruby>は、うたったり、おどったり、おしゃべりする
のがすきなんだって。それもいいよね、だってすきなこと
って、みんなそれぞれちがうでしょ!?

I do my best to be the best version of me.

わたしは自分らしくいられるように、思いっきりがんばる！

I do not compare myself to the other children
I see. I am proud of who I am and free to be me.

ほかの子とくらべたってしょうがないでしょ。大切なのは、あ

りのままのじぶん。

Some children will say things and make you feel sad.

だれかがあなたをかなしませるようなことを言ったりするかもしれない。

Don't give power to their words and continue to be glad.
でも気（き）にしないで。笑（わら）っていて。

Let's support one another to be the best we can be.

みんながじぶんらしくいられるように助け合おう。

Everyone is unique in their own special way.

あなたってそんざいは一人<ruby>一<rt>ひとり</rt></ruby>だけ。それだけでと

くべつなことなんだよ。

Be happy with who you are and what you see.

じぶんでいられること、じぶんだから感<small>かん</small>じられることを、
大切<small>たいせつ</small>にしよう。

It doesn't matter where in the world you are from, nor the colour of your skin, BE you na d do what makes you happy from within.

どこから来たか、はだの色なんてかんけいない。あなたらしく、あなたが楽しいと思うことをしよう。

The moment you feel the butterflies
inside and have a smile on your face,
do more of that to make you grin.

心<ruby>こころ</ruby>がおどるようなこと、えがおになれ

ることをもっとやろう。

One thing to remember
in order to be happy
from within...

もっとじぶんをすきになる
方法（ほうほう）をおしえてあげる。

**Look at yourself in the mirror and say out loud
"I am the best version of me and happy within my skin."**

かがみの中^{なか}のじぶんを見^みて、大^{おお}きな声^{こえ}で言^いってごらん。「

わたしはさいこうよ！」って。

If you believe in and love yourself,
you can achieve anything and win.

じぶんをしんじて、そしてすきでいて！そうした
ら、できないことなんてないよ！

DEDICATION

This book is dedicated to all the children of the world. I made this especially for you so that you are reminded of how amazing you are. Never stop loving yourself, because self-love is the key to happiness.

Special thank you to my daughter Havana and husband Andre for inspiring me to write this. Thank you Naliya for giving me all the happy vibes allowing me to finish writing this book while you were in my belly. Extra special thanks to the most amazing and supportive husband, you are the best thing that happened to me. I love you more than words can describe.

Last but not least...Thank you very much Vanessa for understanding my vision and for bringing it to life through your beautiful images. ¡Muchísimas gracias!

This book is dedicated to Oreofe. Thank you for being part of Havana's life. The world needs more positive books representing amazing, loving and happy boys like you. We love you and your brother dearly.

Being me makes me....

· ·

What about you?
What makes you happy?

LINGO BABIES

Happy Within
Ìdùnnú atọkàn wa.
Copyright © Lingo Babies, 2021

Written by Marisa J. Taylor
Illustrations: Vanessa Balleza

ISBN: 978-1-8382473-4-8

Graphic Design: Clementina Cortés
Translation by Seiya Nobuta

Marisa Taylor

Marisa lives in London UK with her husband and two daughters. They are a mixed Jamaican, Canadian & German family. London has a diverse range of people, cultures & ethnic backgrounds. However, she still found it difficult to find books that represent kids from all over. She is passionate about learning & teaching languages as it is a key element to connecting with people from other cultures. Her desire is to inspire and motivate children from all nationalities & backgrounds to love who they are and help provide resources to be happy within.

To learn more follow her on Instagram @lingobabies

Vanessa Balleza

Illustrator of children´s books based in Florida, Vanessa is passionate about story telling and teaching using her talents to help instil positivity. She has a beautiful and incredible ability to capture anyone´s vision and bring it to life with art, by adding her unique touch of imagination.

To learn more follow her on Instagram @vanessaballezaa

Printed in Great Britain
by Amazon

82722731R00025